Don't Eat the Marshmallow... Yet!

Don't Eat the Marshmallow... Yet!

THE SECRET TO SWEET SUCCESS IN WORK AND LIFE

Joachim de Posada
and Ellen Singer

B

BERKLEY BOOKS, NEW YORK

THE BERKLEY PUBLISHING GROUP
Published by the Penguin Group
Penguin Group (USA) Inc.
375 Hudson Street, New York, New York 10014, USA
Penguin Group (Canada), 90 Eglinton Avenue East, Suite 700, Toronto, Ontario M4P 2Y3, Canada
(a division of Pearson Penguin Canada Inc.)
Penguin Books Ltd., 80 Strand, London WC2R 0RL, England
Penguin Group Ireland, 25 St. Stephen's Green, Dublin 2, Ireland (a division of Penguin Books Ltd.)
Penguin Group (Australia), 250 Camberwell Road, Camberwell, Victoria 3124, Australia
(a division of Pearson Australia Group Pty. Ltd.)
Penguin Books India Pvt. Ltd., 11 Community Centre, Panchsheel Park, New Delhi—110 017, India
Penguin Group (NZ), Cnr. Airborne and Rosedale Roads, Albany, Auckland 1310, New Zealand
(a division of Pearson New Zealand Ltd.)
Penguin Books (South Africa) (Pty.) Ltd., 24 Sturdee Avenue, Rosebank, Johannesburg 2196,
South Africa

Penguin Books Ltd., Registered Offices: 80 Strand, London WC2R 0RL, England

This book is an original publication of The Berkley Publishing Group.

The publisher does not have any control over and does not assume any responsibility for author or third-party websites or their content.

Copyright © 2005 by Joachim de Posada, Ph.D., and Ellen Singer.

First edition: September 2005

Library of Congress Cataloging-in-Publication Data

Posada, Joachim de.
    Don't eat the marshmallow—yet! : the secret to sweet success in work and life / Joachim de Posada and Ellen Singer.
        p. cm.
    ISBN 0-425-20545-2
    1. Finance, Personal—Psychological aspects. 2. Wealth—Psychological aspects.
I. Singer, Ellen. II. Title.

HG179.P575 2005
650.1'01'9—dc22   2005048064

PRINTED IN THE UNITED STATES OF AMERICA

10   9   8   7   6   5   4   3   2   1

Joachim:

To my daughter, Caroline, who has implemented the marshmallow principle with passion, perseverance and courage since the day I first taught it to her. She is the greatest daughter in the world, and I am very proud to be her father.

Ellen:

To the most remarkable women I know, whose combined wisdom and spirit inspire me in all great endeavors . . . my daughters.

Acknowledgments

Joachim:
This book is inspired by the work of Daniel Goleman's *Emotional Intelligence*, which challenged the notion of standard intelligence testing as an indicator of success. Goleman's theory gave me new insight into and appreciation of Dr. Walter Mischel's "marshmallow study," carried out during the 1960s at Stanford University. These two works improved my life dramatically as, I hope, this book will change yours. Thank you to both of these innovative thinkers and to the following important people:

Ellen Singer, who liked this project so much that she brought it to the attention of her (and now our) literary agents, Jane Dystel and Miriam Goderich.

Our publisher, The Berkley Publishing Group, a division of Penguin Group (USA), Inc., for their faith in this project. Denise Silvestro is an excellent editor and her assistant, Katie Day, is extraordinarily helpful. It has been a pleasure to work with both of them.

The University of Puerto Rico for accepting me as a student when so many of my friends were not granted admission.

The University of Miami, where I have taught since 1985. Special thanks for all the opportunities that I have been given by everyone at that wonderful educational institution and their continued faith in me.

The late Dr. Ronald Bauer, an exceptional educator and visionary, who encouraged me, in our last luncheon meeting before his death, to write this book.

Michael LeBoeuf, author of many exceptional business books, for his friendship and everything he has taught me.

The late Sam Walton, who started a small business and in a few years converted it into a gigantic corporation, Wal-Mart, now the largest employer in the world. He is a true example of the wisdom of marshmallow resistance.

My clients all over the world for allowing me to teach the marshmallow principle and encouraging me to convert the teachings into a book.

I would also like to add a final thank-you to everyone who has inspired me and shared ideas that I have absorbed and tried to teach others. My apologies to anyone I have not named individually. I would be happy to give you credit on my website, www.askjoachim.com, and invite you to e-mail me at this address.

Ellen:

I give immeasurable thanks to my coauthor, Joachim, not only for sharing a great writing project but also for introducing me to a marshmallow-resistant lifestyle; to my literary agent, Jane Dystel, for her long-ago faith, continued support and sustained trust in me; to my entertainment attorney, Scott Schwimer, whose intellect and talent are sur-passed only by his wit and compassion; and to my editor, Denise Silvestro, for making helpful—and painless—improvements to the manuscript.

Contents

Pre-Parable Analysis

Born into great wealth but plunged into poverty as a teen, I grew up knowing more about the perils of losing success than the secrets of attaining it. Although my parents recovered after being stripped of everything in midlife, they never regained a prosperous mind-set, and I absorbed their fears more fully than their successes. Those fears fueled my desire to be financially successful and were, in part, what drove me to make a living out of teaching people how to achieve. I grew up to be a motivational speaker who inspired thousands of business executives and professional athletes to attain their goals using valuable principles of success. But what I didn't realize at the time was that I was leaving out one very important part of the equation.

Then, I read about marshmallows, and it changed my life—as it will yours—forever.

After my family lost everything, things were never the same. My parents were never the same, and I was never the same. I think Dad always feared losing everything again, so he overprotected himself. After he regained his wealth, he still drove an old Chevy. He didn't get a Cadillac until he was eighty-one (and died in that same Cadillac two years later). Subconsciously, I had the same fear, but I reacted in the opposite way by spending everything I made. I lived a very lavish life: I spent money on trips, women, gifts, late-model cars and expensive jewelry, never saving a penny and spending more than I made. I ate all my marshmallows as soon as I got my hands on them.

At this point you might be wondering, why didn't my father stop me? Why didn't he attempt to instill in me the same financial values he had learned? My father never taught me the secret to being a successful person because he didn't understand it himself. He was able to put that secret into practice not because of some formulaic knowledge, but because he feared losing everything again. When you are very rich and you suddenly wake up penniless, you learn very important life lessons, but you don't always have time to think about them, much less teach them to others. Thus the secret of attaining wealth remained a mystery to me—a mystery that I later became determined to solve. I wanted to understand and be able to consistently explain:

- Why some people "make it" and some people do not.

- Why some people are successful, while others fail.

- Why 90 percent of people who reach age sixty-five are not independently wealthy, but have to continue working, depend on Social Security or pray that a son or daughter makes it through medical or law school and can afford to help out during the last years of their lives.

I have been a motivational speaker for more than thirty years. I have spoken in more than thirty countries for some of the best corporations in the world and have built up an extensive client list. I have also been involved with sports, motivating athletes in the National Basketball Association and the Olympics. I have found the same question applies: Why is it that some athletes make it and others do not? It's obviously not just talent or ability. The world is full of talented athletes who never make it, and full of less talented athletes who have made it big.

My desire to find the true secret of success led to more research. In the process, I came upon a psychological study performed by a very prominent American psychologist named Dr. Walter Mischel.

I won't go into details on the study right here because you will read about it in the book, but let me tell you one thing: I found *the secret*—why some people succeed and others fail. I thought the lesson was so important that I decided to write a book about it, with the help of my brilliant coauthor Ellen Singer.

Now hear this: This principle must be taught to everyone. What I'm about to tell you is the difference between being rich and being poor. It's a secret that must be taught to all the children of the world. I taught it to my daughter. I want to teach it to you, so you can pass it on to your children.

This book is for entrepreneurs, company employees and self-employed people. It's for athletes and people who generally want to get ahead in life. It's for teachers, who have such an awesome responsibility in educating our youngsters. And yes, it's for teenagers who are willing to change their behavior in order to succeed in life.

But before you move on to the marshmallow parable, here's a question:

There were three frogs that were floating down the river on top of a leaf. One of them decides to jump into the river. How many frogs are left on top of the leaf?

Most people will answer that two remain.

Wrong answer.

There are three frogs left on top of the leaf.

Why?

Because deciding to jump and jumping are two different things.

How many times have you decided to lose weight and found that three months later, the numbers on the scale still haven't changed? How many times have you decided to stop smoking and had a cigarette your next night out? How many times have you decided to clean your attic over the weekend, only to find on Monday it looks even worse?

If that sounds like you, I hope that you do decide to read this book and apply what you learn here, and that you will jump (leap!) toward success.

Sir Francis Bacon said, "Knowledge is power." He was right, but he forgot one word to make the phrase foolproof. "*Applied* knowledge is power." If you know and you don't do, you don't know. It is as simple as that.

Read the book and apply everything you learn. Your life will never be the same. I promise.

I learned the secret. I stopped eating all my marshmallows. When you are finished with this book, you will too.

—Dr. Joachim de Posada,
international speaker and author
of *How to Survive Among Piranhas*,
a book that examines the laws of success
(rules you can apply to great benefit,
after you learn how to resist marshmallows)

Parable

1

Marshmallow Eating Is Self-Defeating

Jonathan Patient, normally as serene and confident as the Brooks Brothers suits he favored, was feeling slightly shopworn as he left a tense business meeting. When he reached his limo, he found his chauffeur stuffing the last ketchup-covered bite of a burger into his mouth.

"Arthur, you're eating the marshmallow again!" he admonished.

"Marshmallow?" Arthur was as bewildered by his employer's harsh tone as he was by the publishing mogul's words. (Jonathan Patient was known to be verbally cryptic.) "It was a Big Mac, honest. I can't even remember the last time I had a marshmallow. I didn't even get any Peeps in my Easter basket this year, and I haven't had a fluffernutter sandwich since—"

"Relax, Arthur. I know you weren't eating a real marshmallow. It's just that I spent the morning surrounded by marshmallow-eaters, and I was frustrated to see you doing the same thing."

"I think I feel a story coming on, Mr. Patient. Would you like me to drive while you talk?"

"Please, Arthur. Esperanza is making her world-famous paella—your favorite, as I recall—and I asked her to begin serving in twenty minutes—at one o'clock—which ties into the point of my story, as you'll see."

"So what does a marshmallow have to do with anything, Mr. Patient?"

"Patience, Arthur. You'll find out soon."

Arthur pulled the Lincoln Town Car smoothly into midtown traffic and tucked his nearly solved *New York Times* crossword puzzle behind the passenger-seat visor as Jonathan Patient settled back into the soft leather seats and began:

. . .

"When I was four years old, I participated in what eventually became a famous experiment. I just happened to be the right age at the right time. My father was studying at Stanford—he was working on his master's degree—and one of his professors was looking for preschool participants to help gather research for an experiment about the effects of delayed gratification in children.

"Basically, kids like me were placed in a room, one at a time. An adult came in and placed a marshmallow in front of me. Then she said she had to leave the room for fifteen minutes. She told me that if I didn't eat the marshmallow while she was gone, she would reward me with a second marshmallow when she returned."

"A two-for-one deal. A hundred percent return on your investment! That would be pretty intriguing even to a four-year-old," Arthur mused.

"Certainly. But at age four, fifteen minutes is a long time. And with no one around saying *no*, the marshmallow became awfully hard to resist," Jonathan said.

"So did you eat the marshmallow?"

"No, but I almost ate it about a dozen times. I even licked it once. It was killing me not to eat that marshmallow. I tried singing, dancing—anything I could think of to distract me—and after what seemed like hours, the nice woman finally returned."

"And did she give you . . . a second marshmallow?"

"Absolutely. Those were the two best marshmallows I ever ate."

"But what was the point of the experiment? Did they tell you?"

"Not then. I didn't find out until years later. The

same researchers gathered up as many of the original 'marshmallow kids' as they could—there were about six hundred of us in the first study, I think—and asked our parents to rate us on a series of skills and traits."

"And what did your parents say about you?"

"Nothing. They never got the questionnaire. I was fourteen by then, and we'd moved a few times. But the researchers found nearly a hundred of the marshmallow families, and the results were quite remarkable.

"It turned out that kids who didn't eat the marshmallow—and even those who resisted for a longer time—did better in school, got along better with others and managed stress better than the children who ate the first marshmallow shortly after the adult left the room. The marshmallow-resisters turned out to be vastly more successful than the marshmallow-eaters."

"Well, that certainly describes you," Arthur said, "but I don't get it. How could your not eating a marshmallow at age four turn you into a billionaire Web publisher at age forty?"

"It didn't directly, of course. But the ability to delay gratification of your own free will turns out to be a strong predictor of accomplishment."

"But why?"

"Let's get back to my original comment when I saw you eating that Big Mac. Weren't you the one who told me this morning that Esperanza promised to save a nice dish of paella for your lunch today?"

"Actually, she promised me the *best* serving, the one with the most *langosta*—but I wasn't supposed to tell you that."

"And what were you doing thirty minutes before she would have served you the best paella in town?"

"Eating a Big Mac—eating the marshmallow! I get it. I couldn't wait to eat, and I spoiled my appetite with something that I could get any time."

"That's right. You went for instant gratification rather than hold out for something you really wanted."

"Gee, Mr. P, you're right. But I still don't get the big picture. Does eating or not eating marshmallows really have anything to do with the fact that you're sitting in the back of the car, relaxing, while I'm up here driving?"

"Yes, Arthur, it makes all the difference in the world. But I'll explain it more tomorrow when you take me back into the city at nine. We're home now, and I'm on my way to enjoy a delicious lunch. What are your plans, Arthur?"

"To avoid Esperanza until I'm hungry again."

• • •

Arthur dropped off Jonathan Patient, opening both car and house doors for the man who'd handed him paychecks and, when he listened, valuable lessons for five years. He didn't know why yet, but he suspected that the marshmallow lesson would prove the most important of all. Without pondering it further, Arthur exited the estate, drove to a nearby grocery store and purchased a bag of marshmallows.

Successful People Keep Their Promises

"Good morning, Mr. P. I hope you're going to keep your promise about explaining the marshmallow story. I can't stop thinking about it."

"I'll explain as much as we have time for on our way into the city, and as much as you want to know on every drive thereafter. Successful people don't break their promises." Jonathan slid into the backseat as Arthur held the door open for him.

"Really, Mr. P? Seems in business all you hear about is people lying and reneging on deals."

"That's true, Arthur. And some people make a lot of money without honoring their commitments. But sooner or later, it catches up with them. People are more likely to produce the results you want if they trust you. But that's another story. And, Arthur—"

"Yes, Mr. P.?" asked Arthur, still standing with the rear door open.

"We'll get to the marshmallow story faster if you get inside the car."

"Oh, ha! Right, Mr. P." Arthur donned his cap, hurried around the car and started its engine.

"Well, Arthur, as I recall, you wanted to know how to apply the marshmallow theory. You wanted to know why marshmallow-resisters are more successful than marshmallow-eaters."

"Yes, I want to know if that's the secret to your success and my, er, limited fulfillment."

"*Limited fulfillment.* That's a clever phrase. I can see why you do well on those crossword puzzles you solve during your downtime."

"Thanks, Mr. P. I've always been good with words. Not that I get much chance to use them."

"You can change that, Arthur, and I'm going to show you how. But first, let's get back to your earlier marshmallow-eating days. We'll start in high school. What kind of car did you drive?"

"Oh, man, Mr. P, I had the hottest car! It was a cherry-red Corvette convertible, a guaranteed babe magnet. I even got the homecoming queen to drive around with me in that car."

"And is that why you bought it?"

"To get hot girls? Absolutely! And it worked too. My little black book was *full*, from Angelica to Zoe."

"I believe you. How did you pay for the car, Arthur? Was it a gift?"

"No, I used the money I got for my sixteenth birthday party for the down payment. Then I had to get a job to afford the monthly payments and insurance and a second one so I had enough money to spend on all the girls who wanted to date me. Then, if the car needed repairs, I was really in trouble, begging my bosses for extra hours so I could get the car fixed before the weekend. I was broke most of the time."

"That 'Vette of yours was a pretty big marshmallow, wasn't it?"

"Huh? What? Oh . . . it was that instant gratification thing, wasn't it? I had to have the best car and the hottest girls immediately. And they're all long gone. Today, I don't even have a car—I drive yours—and none of the classy ladies are interested in a guy who wears a driving cap. This is depressing, Mr. P. But doesn't every guy in high school want hot cars and hot girls? Didn't you?"

"Of course I did, Arthur. I often envied guys like you in high school. Do you know what kind of car I drove in high school? A ten-year-old Morris Oxford. It was the cheapest transportation I could find—in fact, it cost me three hundred and fifty dollars. But it got me back and forth to my job and school and even carried the occasional willing girl on a date. Neither the car nor I were 'babe magnets,' as you call them, but I chose to save my money for college, believing that education was the key to getting *all* the nice things in life I wanted. I didn't eat the marshmallow and look what I got instead."

"About a gazillion marshmallows, Mr. P. Including some mighty tasty-looking marshmallows of the feminine variety, soft and fluffy in all the right places—when you were single."

"Yes, Arthur, you're right," Jonathan said with a chuckle, "although that wasn't exactly the example I had in mind. Try this one. If I offered you one million dollars today or the sum of a dollar doubled every day for thirty days, which would you choose?"

"Mr. P, I am no dummy. I would go for the million bucks. Don't tell me that you would go for the damn buck doubled every day for thirty days!"

"Again, Arthur, you ate the marshmallow. You go for what is obvious instead of thinking long-term.

"You should have taken the dollar. If you had done

that, you would have more than five hundred million dollars, yet you settled for a mere million."

"I can't believe it, Mr. P, but I know you don't ever lie to me, so it must be true."

"Yes, Arthur, that's the amazing power of resisting a marshmallow. Five hundred million dollars in a month is a whole lot better than one million dollars in a day."

"OK, Mr. P. I think you're starting to convince me, but what do I do with the theory? How can I apply it to my life, and how do you apply it to yours?"

"We're almost at the office, Arthur, so I can't answer both questions completely. But let me give you a quick example. Remember, yesterday, when I grumbled that the people in the meeting were all marshmallow-eaters, and how we got started on this conversation?"

"Of course. I think it's the first time I've ever seen your tie out of place."

"We were negotiating a deal to sell our e-sales training courses to a major Latin American corporation. They wanted to buy one course from us that, because of the company's size, would have meant a one-million-dollar deal. I was pushing, as I always do, to sell a more complex package of services, courses and seminars that would have meant establishing a long-term relationship with the company—ten million dollars to start and an important connection in the Latin American market."

"So, what happened?"

"The president of the company was out of town, and we got a call from the vice president, who wanted to meet with us. Our vice president of sales went for the sale when *their* vice president told him exactly what he wanted, which was the one-million-dollar package. What he should have done was to get away from the easy solution and start probing to find out other needs they have. He went for the marshmallow, Arthur, instead of developing a business case strong enough for us to get the ten-million-dollar deal. This happens all the time, Arthur, in many companies all over the world."

"So you got the one-million-dollar deal. Not what you wanted, but not horrible, right?"

"Nothing's been signed. And it gets worse. Yesterday the president of the company calls me and wants to know why we backed out of the long-term relationship. He thought I'd broken my word. He was insulted, believing we'd lost confidence in him, and was opposed to signing any deal with a company that would only think of immediate gain and would not find a solution that exactly met their needs."

"He didn't want to deal with marshmallow-eaters!"

"Exactly. We may have lost the ten-million-dollar deal *and* the one-million-dollar deal because we ate the marshmallow!"

"Can you fix it?"

"That's what I'm about to find out, Arthur. But in any event, it's going to be a long day, possibly a long night. You can go on back to the house, and I'll call you if and when I need you to pick me up today."

"Good luck, Mr. P. I'll be rooting for you!"

"Thank you, Arthur."

Arthur drove back to the Patient estate, parked inside the six-car garage and walked back to the carriage house that he lived in, rent-free, as part of his salary. His life was pretty comfortable. Low-stress job, no major expenses. But after five years, what did he have to show for it? Nothing in the bank and about sixty bucks in his pocket. And no plans that extended beyond next week.

Arthur sighed, entered his modestly furnished home and picked up the bag of marshmallows he'd purchased the day before. He ripped open the plastic bag and started to pop one into his mouth, then stopped and set it on his nightstand.

If it's still there in the morning, he told himself, I'll have two.

Exercising Marshmallow-Resistance

The Importance of Trust and the Power of Influence

When Arthur awoke the next morning, he took another marshmallow out of the bag and thought about eating both of them, then decided to wait instead. He could either eat both when he got home at night or eat four the next morning. Right now he was hungrier for more information from Jonathan Patient, and he had at least an hour's drive to collect it. His employer had spent the night in the city and was waiting for Jonathan to take him to a crosstown appointment.

"You're looking good, Mr. P. Did you kill some marshmallow-eaters last night?"

"No, but I may have converted a few of them. The president of the Latin American company and I had a long talk—I even told him my marshmallow story—and he said he'd agree to the ten-million-dollar deal if I promised to include the story in the series of courses!"

"That's terrific, Mr. P. I'm impressed. You took a million-dollar deal, turned it into a ten-million-dollar deal, then watched it revert to a million-dollar deal, then to a zero-dollar deal, then back up to a ten-million-dollar deal. Talk about multiplying your marshmallows!"

"Thanks, Arthur. I'm very pleased. And if you'd like to listen, I have another story to tell you today."

"Absolutely, Mr. P. Does it have anything to do with the marshmallow theory?"

"I'll tell the story, Arthur, and I'll let you decide. You can do the post-anecdotal analysis."

"Post-anecdotal analysis—the PAA. I like that. Go on, Mr. P."

"Several years ago, I had the pleasure of meeting Arun Gandhi, the grandson of the great Mahatma Gandhi."

"Now, there's someone who didn't eat the marshmallow. He often didn't eat *anything* in order to get what he wanted."

"You're right, Arthur. And Mahatma Gandhi was

very modest about his peaceful accomplishments. Do you know what he once said about the secret to success?"

"No, but you're going to tell me, aren't you, Mr. P?"

"If I remember the quote correctly, it was something like this: '*I claim to be no more than an average man with below average capabilities. I have not the shadow of a doubt that any man or woman can achieve what I have if he or she would put forth the same effort and cultivate the same hope and faith.*' "

"Effort and faith. Do you believe that, Mr. P?"

"Yes, I do. Both are longer paths to success, but both are filled with greater promise and reward."

"Mega marshmallows! So what happened when you met the grandson?"

"He had great respect for Mahatma, of course, and said his father had sent him to live with his grandfather from the time he was twelve until he was thirteen and a half."

"My mom would have loved to send me someplace—anyplace—when I was that age."

"Yes, I'm sure my father would have liked to have done the same. Prepubescent boys are a handful. Arun told me he learned a great deal from Mahatma about discipline and about the wise use of power—how Mahatma collected money for his autograph (he understood the value of his signature) and gave the money to the poor—but credited his own father with teaching him the most valuable lesson a few years later, when he was seventeen.

"He said his father asked him to drive him to a meeting at an office building about fifteen kilometers—nine miles—from his home. When they got there, his father said that he needed him to take the car to the repair shop, wait for the car to be fixed and return to pick him up at five P.M., no later. He was very specific about this; he'd been working long, tiring days and wanted to leave the office at precisely five o'clock.

"Arun said he understood and took the car to the repair shop. At noon, he was going to go have some lunch and then come back, but the mechanic handed him the keys, saying the car had been fixed."

"Uh-oh, a seventeen-year-old, a car and five hours to spare is not a good combination," Arthur said.

"Exactly. Arun started driving around town, spotted a movie theater and went inside to watch a double feature. He became engrossed in the films and didn't even consider looking at his watch until the second it ended—at 6:05 P.M. He ran to his car and hurried to his father's building to pick him up. There his father stood, all by himself, waiting for his son to arrive.

"Arun hopped out of the car and apologized for his tardiness.

" 'Son, what happened to you? I have been worried about you. What happened?'

" 'It was those stupid mechanics, Dad. They couldn't find out what was wrong with the car and they just finished fixing it right now. I came as soon as they finished.'

"Arun's father was silent. He didn't tell his son that he'd called the shop himself at five-thirty because he'd been worried about Arun's well-being, and that he knew the car had been ready at noon. He knew his son was lying. What do you think he did next?"

"Beat the hell out of him?"

"No, but that's what I thought too."

"Grounded him for a week and never let him use the car again?"

"No."

"Tell him he couldn't see his girlfriend or talk to her on the phone for a month?"

"No."

"OK, I give. What did he do?"

"The father handed Arun the keys to the car and said, 'Son, go home with the car. I have to walk home.' "

"What?" Arthur said.

"That's what Arun asked his father. It was a fifteen-kilometer walk. Now, wait until you hear the father's response: 'Son, if in seventeen years I have not been able to build your trust in me, I must be a very bad father. I must *walk home to meditate on how I can be a better dad, and I ask forgiveness from you for being such a bad father.'* "

"You're kidding! Did the father actually do this? Or was he pulling a dramatic guilt trip on the kid?"

"The father started walking. Arun got into the car, started driving, pulling up right next to his father, begging him to get into the car. The father refused and kept walking, saying, *'No, son. Go home, go home.'* Arun drove next to his father the entire way, asking him over and over again to please get in the car. The father refused each time, and the two got home nearly five and a half hours later, at eleven thirty that night."

"That's astounding. What happened next?"

"Nothing, the father just walked into the house and went to bed. So I asked Arun what he learned from this incredible experience and this is his answer: *'I have never lied to another human being since.'* "

"Wow, Mr. P. That's incredible."

"Isn't it, Arthur? I learned many important lessons from that story."

"Tell me, Mr. P—please."

"I will, but first, tell me what you learned. And is it relevant to the marshmallow theory?"

Arthur was uncharacteristically quiet for several minutes. They were nearly at their destination when he spoke:

"The easy solution to the problem would have been to yell, threaten, hit—to punish the kid. If I'd been the father, that's what would have felt good at the time. That's what would have been instantly gratifying. But in terms of teaching the kid a lesson, it would have been like eating the marshmallow. The father venting, the son repenting . . . then both would forget the incident almost immediately. Let's face it: There are lots of worse things the son could have been doing in the car that day. If his father had whacked him for being late and lying, he would have felt punished. Maybe sorry, maybe resentful, maybe afraid, but the incident would have been just another regular screwup that teenagers commit. But because the father delayed his gratification—and I still don't know how he had that much self-control—he had a major, lifelong influence on his son. Is that it, Mr. P?"

"There's no *it*, Arthur. But I agree. The story demonstrates poignantly how much willpower can be required to avoid eating the marshmallow, but at the same time how much impact we can have if we avoid the temptation and focus on long-term rewards."

"What else did you learn, Mr. P?"

"That we can't control other people and can't control most events. But we *can* control our own behavior. And the way we behave can have an enormous impact on the way other people behave, and what we do about an event or how we react is more important than the event itself. Setting an example gives us a tremendous power of influence—the power of persuasion. And that's the most powerful tool to success."

"Can you explain that, Mr. P?"

"Certainly, Arthur. Sooner or later, every successful person realizes that to get what you want from other people, they must have a desire to help you. There are only six ways to get other people to do things: by law, because of money, by physical force, by emotional pressure, physical beauty or by persuasion. Of all these ways, persuasion is the most powerful. It takes you to another level. Arun Gandhi's father persuaded his son to be honest for the rest of his life. I persuaded the Latin American corporate president to sign on to a ten-million-dollar deal and, I hope, persuaded my vice president of sales to stop eating marshmallows."

"That's cool, Mr. P. We're just about at your next appointment. I sort of wish there'd been more traffic so you could have told me more stories. I've been taking notes—not while I'm driving but when I go home. Could you give me something to sum up what you've talked about today?"

"Sure, Arthur. You can write this down: Successful people are willing to do things that unsuccessful people are not willing to do. That's my philosophy, and tomorrow I promise at least one more story to illustrate it."

• • •

When Arthur returned home, he glanced at the two marshmallows sitting on his night table and smiled because, even though he was hungry, he was not tempted to eat them—he wanted to see how many he could accumulate. Then he pulled out a notebook and jotted down the things he had learned, sorting them into categories:

- **Don't eat the marshmallow right away. Wait for the right moment so that you can eat more marshmallows.**

- **Successful people don't break their promises.**

- **A dollar doubled every day for thirty days equals more than $500 million. Think long-term.**

- **To get what you want from people, they must have a desire to help you and they must trust you.**

- **The best way to get people to do what you want is to influence them.**

- **Successful people are willing to do things that unsuccessful people are not willing to do.**

What Successful People Are Willing to Do

"So, Mr. P," Arthur started without preamble as soon as Jonathan was seated in his usual spot in the back of the Town Car, "give me some examples of what successful people are willing to do that unsuccessful people are not willing to do."

"Good morning, Arthur."

"Good morning, Mr. P. I wasn't meaning to be rude. I'm just very excited to learn more about what it takes to become successful."

"I'm glad to hear that, Arthur, and I took no offense. I'll try to give you two examples this morning on our way into the city."

"Thank you, Mr. P."

"Are you familiar with Larry Bird?"

"The great Boston Celtics player? Of course."

"Late in his career, long after his stellar reputation had been established and even when playing a subpar team, he made it a habit to arrive hours before anyone else so he could perform an elaborate ritual."

"What was it, Mr. P?"

"He'd dribble the ball slowly, up and down the court, his head down the whole time. Why? He was checking every inch—every inch—of the court to make sure he would know where the imperfections were so that if he had the ball and they were ahead by one point or behind by one, he would never lose control of the ball by bouncing it in a spot on the court that might deviate it."

"Every game? That's incredible."

"Isn't it? Here's a man who was making millions of dollars, out on the court all by himself, doing what nobody else does. He was successful because he was willing to do what unsuccessful people are unwilling to do. Larry Bird had no outstanding single skill as a basketball player with the exception of shooting the ball. As a jumper, he might have been ranked 253 in the league, as a runner, maybe 146. There was no skill at which he was better than anyone else. Yet he is one of the best fifty players in the history of the game.

"He was willing," Jonathan continued, "to work harder—and smarter—than anyone else, and he achieved success that other, more naturally gifted players could not. They even say that he would shoot three hundred foul shots a day for practice."

"And you said he still did this even after he was on top? At a time when he could have been sitting around eating marshmallows by the bagful and still earning his multimillion-dollar salary? That's impressive. He could have coasted into retirement, but he didn't."

"That's right. He treated every game like the first, took every opportunity to practice as seriously as any other—even when the competition didn't merit the effort."

"I think there's time for another example, Mr. P, if you're up to it."

"I have another sports example. I've seen you wearing New York Yankees hats before. Are you a fan?"

"I go to the games every time I have a chance."

"Then you've heard of the catcher Jorge Posada?"

Arthur nodded.

"When Jorge was much younger, his father, Jorge Luis, asked him if he wanted to make it to the big leagues. Jorge Luis is a scout for the Colorado Rockies and also played on Cuba's Olympic team, so he knows baseball and other sports well.

" 'Yes, Dad, I want to be a pro baseball player, and I want to play in the big leagues,' Jorge said.

" 'Well, son, from tomorrow on, you will be a catcher.'

" 'Dad, I am a second baseman, not a catcher!' Jorge protested. Jorge pleaded with his father to let him play second base, but his father refused.

" 'If you want to be a big-league baseball player someday, you must play catcher. I know what I am saying.'

"Jorge accepted this and the next day he became a catcher. The manager of the team Jorge was playing on at the time didn't want a catcher and kicked him off the team. He had to look for another team on which to play. Finally, a team accepted him as backup. One day, the regular catcher hurt his knee and Jorge started playing catcher. He wasn't very good, but he had the ability and the manager was willing to teach him.

"Another day, Jorge Luis asked his son if he still wanted to go the major leagues and Jorge said yes.

" 'Well, then, tomorrow you start batting left-handed.'

"Once again, Jorge argued with his father. 'Dad, I'm right-handed.'

" 'If you want to make it in the big leagues, you must be a switch-hitting catcher.'

"Jorge agreed. He started batting left-handed and struck out sixteen times in a row (according to Jorge—twenty-three according to his dad) until he had a hit.

"In 1998, Jorge batted nineteen home runs and seventeen were left-handed. In the year 2000, he hit a home run from the left and from the right in the same game. Bernie Williams did the same thing, making it the first time in history that two players from the same team accomplished that. Jorge hit twenty-eight home runs in the year 2000, and along with Derek Jeter, Bernie Williams and Mariano Rivera, he made it to the All-Star Game. In 2001, he hit twenty-two home runs. In 2003, he also made it to the All-Star Game and signed a fifty-one-million-dollar contract. Best of all, he hit thirty home runs, tying Yogi Berra's record of most home runs by a catcher in Yankee history."

"And I know why, Mr. P—because he was willing to do what unsuccessful players are unwilling to do."

"That's right. He was willing to become a catcher when he thought he should be a second baseman; he was willing to learn how to bat left-handed although he was born right-handed. In order to become successful, he was willing to make choices and sacrifices that unsuccessful people are unwilling to do."

"I appreciate you telling me all of this, Mr. P. I'm still trying to figure out how to apply it to my own life. And I also have a concern. In that marshmallow study, you and the other kids were four to six years old, and whether you ate the marshmallows way back then seemed to determine your future success. So, what about kids—and grown-ups like me—who've proven to be marshmallow-eaters in the past (or present)? Can we become successful too, or are we doomed to eat every marshmallow put in front of us for the rest of our lives?"

"If I believed that, Arthur, I wouldn't be telling you these stories. Certainly, it's easier to resist eating marshmallows as an adult if you've practiced that delay in gratification all your life. But it would also be easier to be a switch-hitter if you were born ambidextrous than if you were born right- or left-handed. Success doesn't depend on your past or current circumstances. Success depends on your willingness to do what's required to become successful, and the day you act on that willingness is your first step toward success. The important word is *now*."

"That's good to know, Mr. P. It's not what you've done in the past, it's what you're willing to do in the present that determines your future."

"Yes, Arthur. So, that's a question you'll have to ask yourself: What am I willing to do today to become successful tomorrow?"

"You've given me a lot to think about, Mr. P. And I'll have to do a lot of it without you. Are you still leaving for Buenos Aires in the morning?"

"Yes, Arthur, I'll be gone for five days. We'll have a lot to talk about when I return."

• • •

Arthur wrote in his notebook that night:

Success doesn't depend on whether you've been a marshmallow-eater or a marshmallow-resister in the past. Success depends on what you are willing to do today in order to become successful tomorrow.

Arthur looked at the four marshmallows sitting on his nightstand. Tomorrow, he would have eight. By the time Mr. P returned, if he didn't eat any, he'd have eight, sixteen, thirty-two, sixty-four, one hundred twenty-eight—one hundred twenty-eight marshmallows. He'd probably have to buy a couple more bags!

Arthur pulled out his wallet and was surprised to find that, on the eve of his next payday, he had nearly $200 left. How was that possible? Most weeks, he was down to his last $20 by the time his next direct deposit registered at the bank, and more than once he'd had to get by on whatever change he could find in the car seats and sofa cushions. Usually, Arthur was baffled by where his money had gone. Now, he was puzzled by where it *hadn't* gone.

• • •

Somehow, it seemed important to find out, so Arthur took out his notebook and made a list:

Money saved eating at home: $70

Arthur hadn't missed one of Esperanza's meals all week. He'd been home more—a lot more—and around at mealtime. For five years, he'd had the luxury of a job that came with a free gourmet meal plan, and yet he normally made two fast-food stops in a day. If he saved $70 every week by eating in, he'd have $3,640 by the end of the year. Arthur hadn't had that much money saved since *before* he spent the money from his sixteenth birthday on that Corvette.

Money saved by not going to bars: $50

Arthur wasn't a big drinker, but he usually stopped off at a club once or twice a week. Two drinks and tip set him back $20, and he was always buying drinks for somebody, a pal or a pretty woman. This week, he'd been so caught up in thinking about marshmallows and how to stop eating them that he'd accidentally accomplished his goal—he'd saved $50 without trying. If he did that every week, he'd have $2,600 by the end of the year.

Money saved by skipping weekly poker game: $50

Arthur had gotten so caught up doing Internet research on Mr. P's computer Thursday night that he'd forgotten about the game. Arthur was a pretty good poker player—he never lost his paycheck like some of the guys did—but he'd be lying to himself if he pretended he always won. He usually brought $100 to the game, and sometimes came home with $200, sometimes came home broke. He probably spent an average of $50 a week playing poker.

· · ·

So, this week, he'd saved $70 in food and $50 each in bar tabs and gambling losses. That added up to $170, which was about right. Last week, he'd have been happy to have $30 in his pocket the night before payday. Amazing. Arthur's big expense this past week had been $1.77 worth of marshmallows.

What if he saved that much money every week? Was it possible? Well, possible, certainly; he'd just proven that. But realistic?

Well, he felt certain he could stick to the eat-at-home plan. Even if he missed meals, the kitchen was always open to him. In two minutes, he could make himself a prime rib, braised pork or Cuban sandwich. What was the point of idling in a fast-food drive-thru lane for five or ten minutes with that kind of food waiting at home?

Yes, he could save the $70 a week in food bills for an annual savings of $3,640.

What about his weekly $50 bar tab? Chances were, he'd still hang out at the bar occasionally, but if he went less often, started letting his buddies buy *him* drinks for a change and skipped the pretty lame attempt at impressing girls, he could easily save $30 a week, which would be $1,560 at the end of the year.

And what about the poker game? Arthur enjoyed them; he didn't want to give them up entirely. But what if he only played half as often? He'd save $1,300 a year.

Arthur added it up:

Food money saved:	**$3,640 a year**
Bar money saved:	**$1,560 a year**
Poker money saved:	**$1,300 a year**
Total:	**$6,500 a year**

Just for fun, Arthur completed one more calculation before putting his notebook away. He counted 66 marshmallows in the bag he'd purchased. At $1.77 a bag, he could buy 3,672 bags or 242,352 marshmallows with his annual savings! Or, perhaps, something more valuable . . .

Arthur's head was full of thoughts as he lay down to sleep that night, but most prominent was Mr. P's assurance that he was not doomed to a life of *limited fulfillment*. What had he said?

Success doesn't depend on your past or your present. Success begins when you are willing to do what unsuccessful people are unwilling to do.

• • •

Arthur had some time to kill the next day before he had to pick up Jonathan Patient from the airport. He drove to an office supply store, purchased a large dry-erase board and hung it in his room. He wrote in large letters a list of the things he had learned in the past week.

- **Don't eat the marshmallow right away. Wait for the right moment so that you can eat more marshmallows.**

- **Successful people don't break their promises.**

- **A dollar a day doubled every day for thirty days equals more than $500 million.**

- **To get what you want from people, they must have a desire to help you and they must trust you.**

- **The best way to get people to do what you want is to influence them.**

- **Successful people are willing to do what unsuccessful people are unwilling to do.**

- **Success doesn't depend on your past or your present. Success begins when you are willing to do things that unsuccessful people are not willing to do.**

Below that, he wrote one question:

What am I willing to do today in order to become successful tomorrow?

And some answers:

- **Eat meals at home.**

- **Spend less money at the bar.**

- **Play poker twice a month instead of once a week.**

- **Think long-term.**

5

Marshmallow Multiplication

Obeying the Thirty Second Rule

Arthur was at the head of the limousine queue when Jonathan Patient returned from Buenos Aires. He leapt out of the seat to grab his employer's bags.

"Welcome home, Mr. P! Did you have a good trip? Did the Argentineans treat you well? Have a chance to dance a few tangos?"

"Hello yourself, Arthur. Buenos Aires was fine, thanks for asking. No, no chance to practice my tangos on this trip. You know, Arthur, come to think about it, Argentineans are going through very rough times. In fact, the marshmallow principle applies to countries as well as to people."

"What do you mean, Mr. P?"

"Well, Argentina is one of the richest countries in

the world in terms of natural resources, yet the country is practically bankrupt. Many years ago, they were the eighth biggest economy in the world. Now they are in bad shape; not as bad as Cuba or Haiti, but in very bad shape."

"Why, Mr. P?"

"Well, Arthur, it is a complicated question. We could say that there are many reasons. Corruption in government is one (although they just elected a new president who says he is going to fix that); poor planning and people who are just not motivated (including those who say they have been 'de-motivated' by their leaders) are also concerns. But most important, Arthur, is that they have spent more than they have produced, a clear case of eating their marshmallows too soon.

"Arthur, look at Japan, Singapore, Malaysia or South Korea. Their economic development has been much superior to many of the countries of Latin America."

"Why, Mr. P?"

"Well, they don't eat all of their marshmallows, Arthur. They save a lot of them. As an American of Cuban descent, I feel for Latin Americans. There are very good people in that part of the world and they have the resources to be very successful. They have about thirty-five percent of the world's resources, yet they are only responsible for about nine percent of the world's productivity. We need to change that, Arthur. And one of my objectives in life is to help them develop and be more successful. The Internet will be a big help in bringing Latin America out of economic hard times. With the exception of Cuba, where ordinary citizens are not allowed to tap in to the Internet, in the rest of Latin America, use of the Internet is growing at an extraordinary pace."

"Mr. P, you are a genius," said Arthur.

"No, Arthur, I am not a genius. It is only common sense and a lot of reading."

"Let me ask you, Mr. P: Are Asians smarter than Latin Americans?"

"No, Arthur. There are very smart people in both places. I think it might have something to do with culture."

"Well, I can certainly see that we are comparing marshmallow-eaters to marshmallow-resisters."

"You are smart, Arthur, you learn fast."

"Thank you, Mr. P. By the way, do you remember a long time ago when you offered me the use of your computer?"

"Yes, why?"

"Well, I hope you won't mind, but I used it while you were gone. I wasn't sure if your offer was still open after all this time. I'm sure sorry if it wasn't."

"As I recall, I said you could use the computer any

time it wasn't in use, as long as you used it responsibly. Does that sound right?"

"Yes, Mr. P."

"Did you use it to search for Internet porn?"

"No, Mr. P!"

"Gamble?"

"No."

"Bid for things you couldn't afford on eBay?"

"No, Mr. P."

"Then I will assume you used it responsibly, Arthur, and you can continue to do so whenever you like."

"Thank you, Mr. P. Uh . . . you're not going to ask me what I used it for?"

"No, Arthur, I trust you to tell me—if you want to—when you're ready. I'm glad you've taken an interest in computers. They're an invaluable source of information."

"So I'm discovering, Mr. P. So I'm discovering."

"Any questions for me? Just before my trip, you were asking about your marshmallow-resisting capabilities. Any more questions along that line?"

"I could use some inspiration."

"I told you before about my father studying at Stanford—that's how I got recruited into the marshmallow study—but I never told you about how he ended up there or what it meant for him to obtain the degree. Back in Cuba, my father had been a successful journalist, author of seventeen books, someone who knew—but was an outspoken opponent of—Fidel Castro.

"When he left Cuba, he was penniless—everything was taken from him—and Mom was pregnant with me. He took any job he could find, but he always saved something from every paycheck, no matter how small. And when he couldn't land a job at a newspaper in the U.S., he opted to change careers. That's when he began applying to universities, eventually landing a scholarship to one of the nation's finest schools, Stanford. He had to keep working in order to afford his studies, but he did both.

"He passed on his principles to me, insisting I open a savings account when I took a job delivering newspapers at thirteen. He also encouraged me to apply to the best schools in the country, which I did. I got both my bachelor's and MBA from Columbia. I was accepted to the school, at least in part, because I told them about the marshmallow concept I'd learned from my father.

"It's pretty easy to land a good job with an MBA from Columbia, and I did. Xerox hired me right after graduation, and I started making good money. Remembering how my father had saved part of his paycheck even when he wasn't making enough to pay for food, I saved ten percent of everything I made. I also participated in the company's 401(k) plan—like many corporations, Xerox matched my contributions with their own—and was having fun, earning promotions and raises. I was comfortable and modestly successful.

"Then I learned about an Internet company that was in trouble, and I had to make a decision: stay with Xerox and continue along an upward corporate path, or risk greater success—and failure—by striking out on my own. Fortunately, I had some friends at Xerox who opted to leave with me. We bought E-xpert Publishing, Inc., and built a company that tapped in to the public's need for Web design and Internet marketing. Then, by tapping in to my experience training executives and salespeople at Xerox, we were able to really expand with Web-based courses. We focused on signing up one large customer, rather than going after a bunch of small ones, which meant millions in profits and name-brand recognition.

"The point of all this, Arthur, is that a lot of people could have done what we did with E-xpert Publishing. There must be hundreds of thousands of training managers in the world who could have adapted their teaching skills to the technical requirements of the Web, and at least half as many with the additional sales expertise to know the power of not eating the marshmallow—gobbling up small clients—but holding out for bigger, more important ones."

"But no one else did."

"We were the first, but there've been many others who've tried since, and there will be many more biting at our heels before long."

"So how do you keep ahead, Mr. P?"

"Well, Arthur, let me show you what my dad gave me when I was very young."

Jonathan took out his wallet and unfolded a little piece of paper. It read:

Every morning in Africa a gazelle wakes up.

> *It knows it must run faster than the fastest lion or it will be killed.*

> *Every morning a lion wakes up. It knows it must outrun the slowest gazelle or it will starve to death.*

> *It doesn't matter whether you are a lion or a gazelle.*

> *WHEN THE SUN COMES UP, YOU'D BETTER BE RUNNING.*

"Wow, Mr. P. That is a hell of saying."

"Yes, Arthur, that is why I have kept it in my wallet for twenty years.

"So, we are ready every day to run faster than our competitors and stay on top of research and market demands."

"What else makes you successful, Mr. P?"

"We always have to obey the thirty second rule. Anyone who masters the thirty second rule will be more successful than people who don't, even if those people are smarter, more talented and better-looking."

"What's the rule, Mr. P?"

"No matter what you do for a living, you are first and foremost in the business of connecting with people. Those people will decide whether to connect with you within the first thirty seconds of meeting you."

"So you either make a good first impression or forget it?"

"Something like that. If people decide that they like you, everything about you is cast in a favorable light. Do you leap around when you get excited? Someone who likes you will regard that as enthusiasm. Someone who doesn't like you will think your leaping is a sign of idiocy. An interviewer who likes you might interpret your good manners as considerate, while one who doesn't like you might label you as weak. If a manager likes you, your self-confidence will be viewed as strength of character. A manager who doesn't like you will consider you arrogant."

"And this is all based on perception?"

"Yes. One person's genius is another person's dumbness. It all depends on how you are pictured in the other person's imagination. Capture the imagination and you will capture the heart. The thirty second rule is one business dictate that you can be glad about, Arthur. You connect naturally with people. It will serve you well always."

"Thanks, Mr. P. That means a lot, especially coming from you."

"Some experts estimate that twenty percent of your financial success comes from your skills, talents and knowledge, while eighty percent comes from your people skills, your ability to connect with other people and gain their trust and respect. Whether you are interviewing for a job, trying to get a raise or selling a product or service, the better you are at connecting with other people, the better your chances of getting what you want."

"That makes sense, Mr. P. I've met a lot of people who said they were smart—and they probably were—but since they were rude or nasty, I didn't put much faith in what they said. And yet I've met other people and, without even questioning their expertise, believed they had something of value to tell me."

"Because you liked them?"

"Yes, because I liked them. And no matter what people say about not making snap impressions or not judging a book by its cover, I think we all do it all the time."

"Of course we do, and you're wise to recognize it. And, as I said, I think you're an expert in the likability department. And, before we arrive home, I want to give you one more example of why I believe anyone, no matter what their past behavior or circumstances, can become successful."

"I'm all ears, Mr. P."

"There was a newspaper vendor who started selling newspapers along the railroad tracks of Caracas. A newspaper salesman in Venezuela—not a glamorous or high-paying position. Well, that person—his last name was De Armas, in case you want to look him up online—recently sold his publishing empire to a Spanish conglomerate for hundreds of millions of dollars. Can you imagine, Arthur? Being the poorest of the poor, and now being among the richest of the rich? Again, Arthur, he didn't eat his marshmallow. He saved a percentage of everything he sold. When he had enough money, he bought his first newspaper stand, and then another, and then another and so on."

"I asked for inspiration, Mr. P, and you sure gave me plenty. Thanks a lot."

"You are more than welcome, Arthur."

"I have some errands to run in town, Mr. P, if you won't be needing me for the next few hours."

"I don't have any plans, Arthur. You go ahead, and I'll see you in the morning."

• • •

Arthur dropped off Jonathan Patient and headed for the bank, where he opened a savings account and deposited $350, money he had left over from his last two paychecks. It was still a couple of days to payday, but with $50 in his pocket, Arthur was certain—for a change—that he wouldn't be broke over the weekend. Then he drove to the library to look at a book on hold for him at the reference desk. It was titled *How to Survive Among Piranhas: How to Get What You Want with What You Have.* Yes, Arthur had learned from Mr. P that you must always read motivational books, listen to motivational cassettes and watch motivational videos. So he was ready to do some motivational reading on the weekend. Since it was a Friday, Arthur would stop off for a drink—just one, even if someone else was buying—then see if Mr. P's computer was available for additional research on colleges and careers.

• • •

While Arthur was gone, Jonathan Patient thought about his chauffeur's new interest in computers and decided it would make sense to simply give him one of his many extra laptops. All of the estate was wired for high-speed Internet access, so Arthur could use the computer whenever, wherever he wanted. Tired, but still wound up from his trip, Jonathan opted to deliver the laptop himself rather than assign the task to one of his staff.

A walk might help him get rid of some leftover stress from the long trip and, if he could drop off the computer before Arthur returned, his driver would have a nice surprise waiting for him.

But Jonathan was the one surprised when he let himself into the carriage house and discovered some remarkable changes: a dry-erase board filled with sayings he had recently shared with Arthur, twelve stacks of ten marshmallows and a scattering of—he counted quickly—eight more. Jonathan did the math quickly in his head. Arthur, it seemed, had been doubling marshmallows for seven days. If he kept this up much longer, Jonathan mused, Arthur's home would soon be swallowed up by marshmallows.

Grinning broadly, Jonathan left without touching anything, carrying the laptop with him. He didn't want to embarrass Arthur by letting him know what he'd seen. One of his staff could return with it later or the next day.

6

A Marshmallow Mind-Set
The Rewards of Delayed Gratification

One week later, Arthur was running new errands—returning marshmallows to several local supermarkets. His little at-home marshmallow-doubling experiment was proving unwieldy—and expensive. After fourteen days, he had nearly 8,200 marshmallows in his room. Fortunately, he'd stopped opening bags midweek and would be able to return more than 100 of the 125 bags he'd purchased.

Although he felt slightly foolish traveling from one grocery store to the next, garnering strange looks and comments from the cashiers, he also felt proud of himself:

- He hadn't eaten any of the marshmallows.

- He'd carried out his experiment without fail for fourteen days.

- He'd spent $225 in marshmallows but by keeping most bags intact and saving the receipts, he'd recovered more than $200. He was putting the $200 directly into his savings account, his third deposit in seven days.

Arthur remained committed to completing his marshmallow doubling for the full thirty days but, thanks to the loan of Mr. P's computer, he'd found a less bulky (and less expensive) way to complete it. By putting a picture of one marshmallow into a document and using the cut-and-paste feature, he could visualize the growth within the confines of his laptop screen. And to keep a record of the growth, he also made a chart:

Day 1	1
Day 2	2
Day 3	4
Day 4	8
Day 5	16
Day 6	32
Day 7	64
Day 8	128
Day 9	256
Day 10	512
Day 11	1024
Day 12	2048

Day 13	4096
Day 14	8192
Day 15	16,384
Day 16	32,768
Day 17	65,536
Day 18	131,072
Day 19	262,144
Day 20	524,288
Day 21	1,048,576
Day 22	2,097,152
Day 23	4,194,304
Day 24	8,388,608
Day 25	16,777,216
Day 26	33,554,432
Day 27	67,108,864
Day 28	134,217,728
Day 29	268,435,456
Day 30	536,870,912

Arthur also began classifying the people in his life as marshmallow-eaters and marshmallow-resisters. This new paradigm proved illuminating, as Arthur found his former alliance with and admiration for the eaters shifting toward the resisters.

For instance, his friend Porfirio was a renowned ladies' man, a new marshmallow on his arm every week.

Arthur had long been envious of Porfirio's scorecard—no one took home *more* women—but now, given a choice, Arthur thought he'd rather have one terrific girlfriend than a dozen instant bed partners. But without changing his dating behavior, how would he ever find one? He couldn't spend the time necessary to develop an important relationship *and* date a lot of women at the same time. You can't save a marshmallow you've already eaten.

He thought about his pal Nicholas. Women adored Nicholas, asking him out all the time. But he turned down most of them, which Arthur had long considered a form of insanity. But now? Nicholas seemed lucky, loved for more than two years by a smart, funny, gorgeous lady whom Arthur had introduced him to. Why did Arthur introduce him to his friend? After dating the woman himself a couple of times, Arthur hadn't been able to resist the next marshmallow he'd met.

Arthur also thought about his poker buddies. Even playing cards, it was possible to resist rather than eat the marshmallow. Eric bet on every remotely winnable hand and tried to force the other players to drop out before they had a chance to beat him. Karim, on the other hand, folded after the first deal more often than not. But when he had a great hand, he never went for the easy win. He'd encourage everyone to keep betting until the pot was huge—then he'd lay down his cards. Karim didn't win as often as the other players in his poker group, but he won the largest amounts. Arthur used to consider Karim a rather boring poker player, but there was nothing boring about winning! Maybe Arthur could learn something from Karim.

Karim held out for bigger jackpots just like Mr. P held out for bigger clients and bigger sales. If Arthur could find a way to apply the marshmallow-resisting theory in both his professional and private life, it would be a major marshmallow coup. Could he do it?

So far, Arthur was saving money—nearly a third of his paycheck—by eating at home and spending less on drinking and gambling. What else could he do? What else was he *willing* to do today in order to become successful tomorrow?

Arthur drove home and started making a mental list:

THINGS I AM WILLING TO DO TO BECOME SUCCESSFUL:
Spend less? Yes. Reduce entertainment expenses.
Save more? Yes. Aim for $200 a week.
Earn more? Yes, but?

Arthur thought more about this when he got back to his house. His driving job left him with a lot of free time, but it also required him to be available to Mr. P 24/7. So he couldn't take a regular job like delivering pizzas—he'd have to drive off with a customer's deep-dish pepperoni if Mr. P called on his cell phone. But there must be *some-*

thing. He'd do some research on this. In the meantime, was there some other way to increase his savings?

Arthur sighed, walked over to his closet and pulled out his baseball card collection. Man, he loved those cards! He'd been a serious collector for about ten years. Some of his cards must be worth hundreds, maybe even thousands of dollars by now. Could he part with them? Was it worth parting with them? Was his reluctance emotional or financial? Something else to think about.

Arthur wasn't very impressed with his list so far. Maybe he needed another approach. Maybe if he defined his goal first, ways to attain it would follow. What had he decided in the past two weeks to be his top priority—the one he was studying on the Internet, checking out at the library and keeping to himself?

Number One Goal: Go to College

Arthur knew college was a must if he was going to become successful in any of the fields that interested him. So what was he willing to do to obtain this goal? Spend less and save more—yes. And he would research other ways of making money—earning more and selling things he didn't need.

But money was not the only thing he needed to go to college. He had to get accepted first. He wrote down a new question:

WHAT AM I WILLING TO DO IN ORDER TO GET ACCEPTED INTO COLLEGE?

- **Study for the SAT ten hours a week.**

Arthur had found sample tests online and books to study from at the library. He could definitely commit to a preparation schedule of two hours a day.

- **Start filling out applications.**

To Arthur's surprise, he could do much of this online, including writing his admissions essays. He could get this task out of the way now, before taking the SAT, so he wouldn't risk missing any application deadlines.

- **Set up interviews at schools that interest me.**

What was it that Mr. P had said about much of success being based on how well you connected with other people? Arthur could make certain his applications got noticed by establishing early contacts with people on the review committees. And, as a twenty-eight-year-old chauffeur with a less-than-stellar academic history, he'd need an edge competing against all those high school seniors with impressive GPAs.

- **Ask Mr. P for a letter of recommendation.**

Arthur added, then crossed this off the list. This wasn't something he was willing to do yet. Maybe later when he could prove to his employer that he was serious, that he had accomplished at least some of his other commitments.

- **Give myself more credit for taking the marshmallow challenge.**

Maybe that one was silly, but Arthur decided to keep it on his list. After all, he'd only been introduced to the marshmallow concept three weeks ago and had already made some dramatic changes. Just a few minutes ago, though, he'd berated himself for the brevity of his "willing to do" list, upset that he couldn't commit to selling his baseball card collection. Staying positive would help him keep focused.

Toward that end, he wrote:

In three more days, I will have a million marshmallows.

7

Marshmallow Mellow
Purpose + Passion = Peace of Mind

"So, Arthur, it's been a few weeks now since we first talked about the marshmallow experiment. Is it having an impact on your life?"

"In more ways than you can believe, Mr. P.," Arthur said as he headed south toward the city. "In fact, I can tell you precisely how many days ago you compared my Big Mac to a marshmallow—twenty-nine!"

"How do you remember so accurately, Arthur?"

"Because the day you introduced me to the marshmallow theory, you also told me about doubling a dollar for thirty days—how you'd end up with more than five hundred million dollars. I thought it would be fun to do the doubling with marshmallows and, as of tomorrow, Day Thirty, I'll have 530,870,912 marshmallows—and if

I doubled it one more time I would have more than *one billion marshmallows*."

"Arthur, please don't tell me you have five hundred million marshmallows stored in the carriage house."

"No, Mr. P, they wouldn't fit. I did the math, and you'd need a space forty by forty by twenty feet to squeeze in that many marshmallows. And don't panic, Mr. P, I stopped using real marshmallows two weeks ago—they were getting expensive—and now I just multiply them on the laptop you loaned me."

"Gave you, Arthur. It's yours to keep."

"Thank you, Mr. P!"

"You're welcome, Arthur. I can see that the laptop was a wise investment on my part. You seem to be finding some imaginative uses for it."

"You'd be amazed, Mr. P. I canceled a date last week because I was negotiating an online deal to sell off some of my baseball cards."

"You gave up a date to trade baseball cards?"

"Not trade—sell, Mr. P. I made more than three thousand dollars by convincing the buyer to take five instead of just a single card. And if I'd sold the entire collection outright to a dealer, I would have made less than two thousand dollars."

"You didn't eat the marshmallow! Congratulations, Arthur! You must have a valuable collection."

"I plan on getting at least ten thousand dollars for it by selling the cards separately or in small lots. I did all the pricing on the Internet and by taking the cards to local dealers."

"Again, I congratulate you. What's your motivation for selling the collection? You're not in financial trouble, I hope?"

"No, just the opposite. I'm saving money, Mr. P, but I'd rather not tell you why just yet."

"Good for you, Arthur. But could I add just one note of caution?"

"Sure, Mr. P."

"I want you to know that I applaud your ambition and motivation, and I'm certain you will achieve every success you intend."

"What's the bad part, Mr. P?"

"There's no *bad part*, Arthur. I just want you to know that everyone—me included—eats a marshmallow from time to time, and I don't want you to be too hard on yourself if you slip up once in a while. Maybe at some point you're going to get tired of selling your baseball cards individually, and you'll unload the rest of the collection for a few hundreds dollars. Maybe you'll make five thousand dollars instead of the ten thousand you've planned. It will be easy at that point to get mad at yourself for forfeiting that five-thousand-dollar potential profit. It's important to focus on your accomplishments—if you make five thousand dollars, that's still three thousand more than if you'd sold them all at once to a dealer and five thousand more than if you'd left them sitting in your closet."

"Thanks, Mr. P. I know what you mean. I had to write a note to myself saying, *Give yourself credit* for when I'm feeling discouraged. But the funny thing is, Mr. P, that the more I focus on my goal and get excited about it, the less stressed I am about achieving it. Each time I delay my gratification and accomplish something toward my goal, I get more confident of my ability to keep doing it. Does this make sense?"

"Yes, it does, Arthur. And since you were mentioning mathematic formulas a few minutes ago, I have one that you could apply here."

"What is it, Mr. P?"

"Purpose + Passion = Peace of Mind."

"I like that, Mr. P. When you have a goal and get excited about reaching it—and do what it takes to reach it—the effect is calming. A few weeks ago, I was overwhelmed with the question of whether I could ever become successful—remember I asked if your ability to become successful was locked in at age four, your age when you participated in the marshmallow experiment? Now that I have a goal and am taking action toward it,

I'm not hung up on the *if*. I'm concentrating on the *how* and *when*."

"Good point, Arthur. Maybe we could modify that proposal: Purpose + Passion + Action = Peace of Mind."

"It's definitely the 'action' part that makes the difference. I think that as long as you're taking action steps— even small ones—you're rewarded with a sense of peace. I started by writing down the question you asked me: What am I willing to do today in order to become successful tomorrow? Each time I added an answer, I felt a little better. Each time I implemented an answer, I felt *a lot* better. Every time I resist eating a marshmallow—like yesterday when I passed a pair of golden arches without pulling into the drive-thru—and hold out for something better, like a prime rib sandwich, it's like getting a shot of endorphins."

"I can't tell you how pleased I am to hear this, Arthur. What began as one frustrated remark by me a month ago seems to have produced some remarkable changes in you. Are you certain you're not ready to tell me yet what your big marshmallow secret is—what your plans are?"

"Not yet, Mr. P. But I promise that, next to me, you'll be the first to know. I'll tell you just as soon as I can."

8

Mushy Marshmallow Stuff

Arthur sat in the Town Car, parked outside the tall office building that housed E-xpert Publishing, struggling to find the courage to go inside. His brow was sweaty, his hands shaky and his mouth felt as dry as if a dental hygienist had turned the aspirator on high.

He had promised to make Mr. P the first person he told of his plans, and he intended to keep his promise. He couldn't wait much longer—his "plan" started in just a few weeks. He couldn't believe it had been eight months since Mr. P had told him the marshmallow story—and changed his life. Nor could he believe how scared he was to face his employer.

He hadn't been this nervous since he'd asked Amy Thompson to his eighth-grade dance. Of all the things Arthur had put on his "willing to do today in order to become successful tomorrow" list, the task immediately ahead of him was by far the hardest and the one he'd put off the longest.

Determined, Arthur exited and locked the car, then rode the elevator up to the sixty-eighth floor. He knew the E-xpert office staff slightly—sometimes Mr. P asked him to move office files to the estate—and was thankful when the receptionist greeted him warmly and waved him into Jonathan Patient's office without question.

"Mr. P, do you have a minute?"

"Of course, Arthur. Come on in. Is anything wrong?"

"Yes and no, Mr. P. I'm here to hand in my driver's cap. I came to officially give you notice that I'm leaving at the end of the month. I'll be happy to help train my replacement and do anything else I can do to ease the transition and—"

"Are you unhappy working for me, Arthur? Have I failed in some way to treat you with the proper dignity and respect?"

"Gosh, no, Mr. P! Nothing could be further from the truth. It's because you have treated me so well and taught me so much that I found the determination to . . . to go to college, Mr. P. I've been accepted at Florida International University."

"That's a wonderful school, Arthur! I'm impressed

and pleased for you. Will you be able to handle it, financially and all?"

"It won't be easy, Mr. P. But in the eight months since you told me about delaying gratification—about not eating every marshmallow put in front of me—I've saved more than fifteen thousand dollars from my paycheck, from the sale of my baseball card collection and from a little business I've started."

"A business, Arthur? What kind of business?"

"After I sold off my baseball card collection, I got to thinking . . . I never cared so much about having the cards, it was the collecting and scoring great deals that I liked. I was looking for a way to give up the cards without sacrificing the pleasure they gave me—and I ended up finding a way to make a little extra income."

"How, Arthur?"

"I've made myself an online broker for baseball card collectors. Basically, someone sets a price he or she wants for a card. If I come within eighty-five percent of that amount, I collect a small fee. But if I can sell it for more— and this is where the real income comes from—I keep anything extra as a bonus. The client's happy—he got his asking price—and I'm real happy when I can negotiate a big sale. It's not enough to make me rich, Mr. P, but it will help pay for books and Big Macs. Without Esperanza's cooking, I'll probably be back to eating those again!"

Jonathan Patient was silent for a moment, then reached into his desk and pulled out an envelope.

"Arthur, you're welcome to drop by for a home-cooked meal anytime and if you call ahead, I'll make certain she cooks a wonderful paella for you—and that you get a good piece of lobster."

"Thank you, Mr. P. But it's not Esperanza's cooking I'm going to miss most, it's you, sir."

"Oh, Arthur, the *sir*'s not necessary. I'm going to miss you terribly too. But I have been preparing for this day. I've watched you change and grow so much. I knew you were going to be successful, that you were willing to do what unsuccessful people are unwilling to do. So, six months ago, I tucked something away for you. Here."

Arthur accepted the envelope Jonathan Patient handed to him.

"Mr. P—it has my name on it!"

"Yes, Arthur, I told you it was for you! And now that you're about to become a business peer, I think it's time you started calling me Jonathan."

Arthur opened the envelope and gasped at what he saw inside.

"Mr. P, Jonathan, it's—"

"Enough to cover four years' college tuition. I know you could accomplish this without my help. In fact it's *because* you've proven that you can accomplish this on your own that I'd like you to accept this gift. You've worked long and hard and deserve this. It's time you enjoyed a marshmallow or two. I also know that one day when you are very successful, you will pay this forward to someone who has potential and needs a little bit of help."

Arthur threw his arms around Jonathan and the two men embraced, tears running down their cheeks.

Post-Parable Analysis

Marshmallow-resistance is more than just a theory—it is a way of life. No matter what your profession, your personal definition of happiness or your conception of an ideal personal or business relationship, resisting marshmallows will bring you success. And it doesn't matter how many marshmallows—or mini-marshmallows—currently lie within your grasp. Anyone can attain marshmallow abundance by following the principles in this book.

And what will be your reward?

You'll be able to send your kids to college. You'll be able to send yourself to college! You'll form more lasting, more lucrative business relationships. And when you retire, you will be able to maintain your standard of living. Is it fair to have worked fifty years and at the end have nothing? If you follow the marshmallow principle, you'll never find yourself in that situation.

S'MORES TODAY . . . BUT NONE TOMORROW

Marshmallow-resistance is not easy or popular. We have become a fast-food society. As a culture, both on the individual and corporate levels, we are always focusing on *instant* gratification, *instant* rewards and, of course, *instant* profits. What we need to do is reconfigure our priorities. You will make millions of choices throughout your life, and each of those choices will determine who you are, what you do and what you become or possess. There are plenty of people who begin life in luxury and end it in poverty, and just as many who spend their early years in "the hood" or a trailer park and achieve millionaire—even billionaire—status. Don't blame (or rely on) your past. It's what you do with your current assets, how you use your talent, education, personality, persistence, money and marshmallow-resisting skills that matters.

So how do you apply the marshmallow principle to your life? Let me share some real-life examples that will help you apply what Arthur learned in the parable. I'll begin with my own experience because if I'd been part of the marshmallow experiment at age four, I'd have eaten my treat before the administrator even left the room!

GREAT CREDIT = GREATER DEBITS

I've made tons of money in my life, but for years I made a habit of spending tons more. I was constantly in debt, frequently without enough cash to pay basic bills. Because of the values taught to me by my mother and father, skipping payments (or filing for bankruptcy) was not an option, so I ended up paying one credit card bill with another credit card—eating marshmallows months before I had earned them. Lending institutions loved me, giving me AAA ratings and a quarter million dollars in available credit, but I hated that my successful façade was disguising real failure. I didn't want to end up like 90 percent of the U.S. population: depending on Social Security, their children or the ability to keep working until they die.

Then I read about the marshmallow experiment, and it changed my life so completely that I felt compelled to share its simple wisdom with the widest possible audience. My change began modestly, and so can yours. I had just been named vice president of a multinational company and was given the option of having a portion of my paycheck deducted and earmarked for retirement savings. I opted for the deduction. Even though I no longer work for that company, I continue to set aside a portion of my earnings every month. I started saving my marshmallows in midlife and guess what? I could retire today and live comfortably for the rest of my life.

MARSHMALLOW CHOICES:
TOAST, ROAST OR COAST?

I am driven to work by my passion to help others. But if I became tired, ill, disillusioned or in need of a new challenge, I could walk away from my speaking engagements and still be financially able to support myself. Do you know how liberating (and what a relief to my daughter) that is? Dr. W. Edward Deming, the quality movement guru, once remarked that he loved his work so much he planned to die in a classroom. As it turned out, at age ninety-two, he was taken from a seminar to a hospital, where he died shortly thereafter. Right now, I have the to-the-grave enthusiasm of Dr. Deming. But if I ever wanted to reduce or even eliminate entirely my workload, I have enough marshmallows saved up to do so.

I recommend that you become a super saver instead

of a super spender. If you save your marshmallows you will reach your goals. Eat your marshmallows, and you will not. The unwillingness to save marshmallows is what keeps people in the money trap. American productivity is very high, but the American savings ethic is very poor. In August 1999, the *Dallas Morning News* reported that 33 percent of all households are plain broke, which means that a third of our population has no cash assets. And a recent survey of 1,200 working Americans as reported by *American Demographics* revealed that almost 40 percent of baby boomers have saved less than $10,000. And there are lots of people who are much worse off!

Imagine millions of people reaching age sixty-five and not having any money left. Who will support them? Even if it doesn't collapse under its own weight, the Social Security system will provide only bare-essentials finances. The aging boomers and the entire U.S. economy would suffer enormously if today's top spenders became tomorrow's neediest population. That's why it's so important that our culture adopt the marshmallow principle.

MERCEDES OR MARSHMALLOW?

Michael LeBoeuf, a good friend and, in my opinion, one of the best business authors in the world, helps us calculate the cost of lost wealth better than anyone else I know. He asks, "Are you driving your financial freedom? Are you wearing it on your wrist, on your fingers or around your neck? Are you eating in fancy restaurants, smoking or drinking it? Are you giving it to your landlord by renting a posh apartment when you could be investing in a home that will appreciate and give you a handsome tax deduction? The true cost of an item isn't merely the out-of-pocket cost. It is the forgone wealth that money compounded over time can earn you."

Here, from Michael, are five reasons to save your marshmallows. Suppose that, instead of spending the following amounts of money, you invested them in an index fund averaging an 11 percent annual return (just under the average annual return of the S&P 500). Here's what you'd find:

1. If you saved instead of spending $5,000 on a wrist-watch at age twenty-seven, you'd have $263,781 by age sixty-five.

2. If you saved instead of bought a dollar a day in lottery tickets starting at age eighteen, you'd have $579,945 by the time you reached retirement age.

3. If you avoided credit card interest charges from adulthood to retirement age, you'd save $1,606,404

(based on $1,440 annual interest charged on an average credit card balance of $8,000).

4. If you saved instead of spent $5 a day on junk food, cigarettes or booze from age twenty-one to age sixty-five, you'd have an extra $2,080,121.

5. If you bought instead of renting a home, at an average of $1,000 a month, you'd save $13,386,696 from age twenty-one to age sixty-five.

DON'T SAY "YES" . . . YET

Apart from saving, how else can you apply the marshmallow principle? For salespeople (and most of us have to sell ourselves even if we are not directly in a sales position), it means learning when and how to say "yes." Here's an example:

I once did a time-management seminar in San Juan that was attended by some people from the Puerto Rico Telephone Company. After the seminar, they asked me to meet with their director of management development, who asked me if I would provide a time-management session for his company. It was tempting to immediately agree, but that would have been eating my marshmallow. Instead I answered, "Yes, I can certainly do a time-management session for your employees, but let me ask you, what problems are you having that you think a time-management session will solve?" The answer to that question resulted in a $1.2 million training contract with the Puerto Rico Telephone Company. Remember this: When a client tells you that he or she wants to buy X product or service, if you open your bag immediately, take out the order form and fill it out, you ate your marshmallow! Instead, find out what else that client might need. That way, instead of eating that one marshmallow, you'll be giving yourself the opportunity to earn many, many more.

MARSHMALLOW PRACTICE: WALL STREET AND BEYOND

Although *Don't Eat the Marshmallow . . . Yet!* has been written for and about business and financial success, I firmly believe that it can be applied to any profession or goal, and to any person at any age. You've probably heard the oft-repeated stories of lottery winners who ended up broke (or worse). You may have harrumphed about the unfairness of sudden wealth being transferred to a person who didn't know how to handle it—shouldn't that lucky ticket have belonged to you instead? Surely you would have done better! But the problem of having and then losing mounds of marshmallows is not limited to people made into instant millionaires by a one-dollar ticket. It also happens to people who spend their lives working hard for their money . . . even people like you and me.

Whether your goal is a promotion within your company, a new car, millionaire status or the reverence of your peers, success hinges on your ability to enjoy but not devour early success, and to act in ways compatible to your goals. The marshmallow principle is not about endless self-denial—the only reason you should die with marshmallows under your mattress is because they help you sleep better! Rather, it's about balancing current and future desires.

It's easier to spend money than to make it, and I know that, often, your appetite is bigger than your bank account. But even a history of success can be undone by a poor fiscal attitude and inappropriate choices. How many times have we watched a wealthy celebrity, CEO or public figure lose everything because of bad financial decisions? The powerful desire to spend—and spend freely—has brought down people who once considered themselves financially invincible. They didn't realize that the true secret to marshmallow success is knowing what you want and keeping the end goal in mind, and doing whatever it takes to achieve your big marshmallow dream rather than gobbling all the mini-marshmallows along the way.

There are many paths to success, but as I hope I've proven to you, true sustainable success can only come with patience, perseverance and a steady eye on one's long-term goal. I'd like to give you a couple of examples to illustrate what I mean.

PIRATES AND PARADISE

Johnny Depp, a high-school dropout reared by a struggling single mom, is now hailed by his peers to be among the most intellectual of actors. He is a clear case of someone who didn't take the easy way to success, handed to him almost immediately upon his arrival to Hollywood. He made his big-screen film debut at age twenty-one in the horror classic *A Nightmare on Elm Street* (his first film role) and three years later was earning $45,000 per episode in a starring role on *21 Jump Street*, which catapulted him to teen-sex-symbol status and kept him there for the three years he remained on the show.

It would have been easy for someone with Depp's humble roots to sit back and enjoy the money and popularity. But Depp, who said he didn't want to become a Hollywood "product," left the show midrun and took a risk by playing the naïve, deformed Edward Scissorhands. The result was Depp's first Golden Globe nomination and opportunities to play other critically acclaimed roles in movies as diverse as *Benny and Joon* and *Ed Wood*.

Early in the new millennium, Depp was offered $10 million to play Captain Jack Sparrow in *Pirates of the Caribbean*. *Pirates* could easily have been a walk-in-the-amusement-park role for Depp: an A-list paycheck for a supporting part. How hard could it be to play a pirate based on a Disneyland ride? Again, Depp showed he was stuffed with more than corn-syrup fluff. He risked getting fired by showing up on set with dreadlock-and-braided hair, gold-capped teeth and the aura of Keith Richards, the Rolling Stones legend on whom Depp based his character. Disney execs were alarmed, but grudgingly allowed the not-ready-to-eat-my-marshmallows actor to play the role his way. Depp's intuition and talent netted him an Oscar nomination, among seventeen others, which led to other awards, including a Screen Actors Guild award.

There's no indication that Depp plans to cash in his marshmallows anytime soon. He avoids easily won publicity and says he would rather spend time playing with "the kiddies" (the daughter and son born to French model and actress Vanessa Paradis) than socializing with the Los Angeles in-crowd. For Depp, success means more than just making money.

"The challenge for me is still to do something that hasn't been beaten into the movie-going consciousness," Depp said in a March 2004 interview with *Time* magazine. "Otherwise what am I in it for?"

THE RUBBER-FACED MAN

Jim Carrey arrived in Hollywood with a hard-knocks family background, little education and only one proven talent: making people laugh. Although Carrey aspired to be more than a funnyman, he knew the way to reach his goal of playing dramatic parts was to first become super successful in comedic roles. Just as my cousin, Jorge Posada, taught himself to be a catcher and a left-handed batter when he fancied himself a second baseman, Carrey made people laugh even when he didn't feel like laughing himself because he believed it was something he could do better than anyone else. Although he was plagued by a bipolar disorder that exaggerated the emotional lows of his early struggles, Carrey kept himself motivated with a trick anyone can replicate: He wrote himself a check for $10 million, postdated it and carried it with him at all times. When he got discouraged, he would pull out the check and envision himself cashing it, imagining the roles he would be offered and the life he would lead when he had $10 million in the bank.

Carrey's vision and his ability to set and stick with a goal paid off. He was able to cash that $10 million check—almost to the date he had written it for—and expand his career from the broad humor of *Ace Ventura* to darker, more sophisticated comedy such as the role he created in *Eternal Sunshine of the Spotless Mind*, which won an Oscar for best original screenplay.

You don't have to have Carrey's rubber face to mold your own success. Determine your ultimate marshmallow reward and keep it within your vision (or tucked inside your pocket) at all times, and the sweet taste of *permanent* success will be yours.

And that success should be the success *you* define— it should be no one's vision but your own. Having to delay gratification and weather the inevitable disappointments you'll face in life is no easy job. The motivation you need to attain and sustain your goals will be bolstered when those goals are firmly rooted within you. Do you think the $10 million check Jim Carrey kept in his pocket would have inspired him if he'd been content to remain a low-paid stand-up comic? It's easy to eat our marshmallows—in the form of money, jobs or relationships—if we don't care about our futures. But when your goals are clear and clearly yours, the marshmallow theory will become a way of life.

IT'S A MARSHMALLOW WORLD

My coauthor, Ellen, and her two daughters have incorporated the marshmallow theory into their daily routines. Now it plays a role in all the decisions they make, both major and minor—they even speak marshmallowese! But less than a year ago, when I first approached Ellen about writing *Don't Eat the Marshmallow . . . Yet!*, she couldn't envision the theory applying to her.

"It made sense to me as a *business* theory, which is how it was first explained," Ellen says, "but I didn't understand—and therefore resented—the application of the marshmallow principle to anyone outside corporate life. As someone who'd recently been down to $1.87 after a jilted lover emptied my bank account, my immediate reaction was a whiny 'But what if you don't have any marshmallows to resist? I *have* to eat the marshmallow; I'd starve if I didn't.'"

However, when Ellen stopped considering the theory only in financial terms, she found it had almost universal applications (and surprising monetary rewards).

"I told my daughters about the marshmallow-resistance theory one day; the next day, my younger one told me what she wanted for her sixteenth birthday. From the list provided, I was convinced she was rejecting both the marshmallow principle and our fiscal reality."

The list included:

- Jimmy Choo shoes (the kind Reese Witherspoon wore in *Legally Blonde*)

- Poppie Harris shirts (Britney Spears buys them ten at a time)

- Juicy Couture hoodies and sweats (not pink like JLo's, but maybe a tan one like Madonna's)

- 7 for All Mankind jeans (Phoebe on *Charmed* wears hers with Manolo Blahnik heels, but Monica on *Friends* wore them with Puma sneakers, so you can dress them up or down)

- MAC makeup (once you try MAC, you can never go back)

- Louis Vuitton bags (Hilary Duff collects them)

- Lexus (if you're going to get a new car, it should be nice, and they're more reliable than a Porsche)

But before Ellen had a chance to protest, her daughter, Allison, continued:

"It's not like I actually expect you to get me any of this, but it is what I *want*. Right now, I'm saving up for a Juicy hoodie—they retail for $100, but they go on sale for half that and they're really comfortable. And if I make enough money this summer (after putting some away for college), I might get a pair of Juicy sweats too, but only if I can get a good deal on them. I really love MAC lip gloss, and it's about $14, but I also saw a sampler set on eBay: six mini lipsticks for $5. And the set comes with a lip brush that MAC sells for $15 all by itself. Shipping on that item is only $2.50. I wouldn't bid higher than $7.50 for the set—$10 total—and you could spend more than that buying lip gloss at Rite Aid without getting anything special."

And the car?

"I don't even have my license yet! And I can walk to school. Maybe I could borrow your car sometimes, though? Cars are really expensive. You definitely don't want to marshmallow a purchase like that."

Marshmallow a purchase?

"You know, eat the marshmallow by paying sticker price or not checking out its repair record or whether it's better to buy used . . . stuff like that."

• • •

When a child turns a noun into a verb and a piece of candy into a catchphrase in less than a month, pay attention! Something very important is going on!

Ellen recalls she only chatted casually with her daughters about the marshmallow theory, just as she talks to them about all of her writing assignments. She was amazed that both immediately embraced the idea of not eating the marshmallow as a way to succeed in business and in life.

"Oh, that's not even a question," said one.

"Everyone will buy into the theory," said the other.

"Why?" asked Ellen, still unconvinced herself.

"First, it's kinda funny. Marshmallows are funny. So it's an amusing way to explain a serious concept. It's a concept that makes sense—it's always better to hold out for what you really want, to get the two marshmallows instead of one."

"And it's not just about business; it's about life. Everyone can apply it."

•   •   •

Ellen's elder daughter, Marina, has also gotten on the marshmallow wagon. Although she's a natural marshmallow-resister who started planning her college career before she started high school, Marina called her mom a month ago and said she wanted to come home.

"For the weekend?" Ellen asked.

"For good," Marina said. "I want to drop out. I'm eating my marshmallows here, and I'm getting discouraged about ever reaching my goal."

Ellen definitely wanted her daughter to stay in school. Marina was halfway through her junior year on a four-year full scholarship. The school's health insurance plan covered her $500-a-month medical costs. And furthermore, college was important! Ellen had earned a master's degree and taught university writing courses and anticipated that her daughters would surpass her educational accomplishments. There was no question about what *Ellen* wanted.

But thanks to the marshmallow theory, Ellen didn't take the easy way out of the problem. Instead, she asked Marina the following questions—questions I advise each of you to ask yourself:

THE FIVE-STEP MARSHMALLOW PLAN

1. **What do you need to change?** What strategies can you implement right now to stop eating your marshmallows? What will you commit to changing?

2. **What are your strengths and weaknesses?** What do you need to improve, and how can you best make these improvements?

3. **What are your major goals?** Pick at least five and write them down. Then write down what you need to do to attain those goals.

4. **What is your plan?** Put it in writing. If you can't see a goal, you can't achieve it.

5. **What are you going to do to put your plan into action?** What will you commit to doing today, tomorrow, next week, next year to help you reach your goals? As Arthur learned in the parable: How will you become willing to do what unsuccessful people are unwilling to do?

For Marina, whose number-one goal was to become an actor, her decision was to take a leave of absence from college. Her commitment is to replace college courses with acting classes, to find an agent, to move to Los Angeles, to apply or audition for at least one role a day, to find a job to support her endeavors—and to complete her college education when acting jobs can pay her tuition.

Ellen says she has no doubt her daughter will fulfill

her acting aspirations, "because she knows what she wants to do, knows what she has to do and is willing to do whatever it takes to achieve her goals. And, because I never prescribe for my daughters what I don't practice myself, I am following the five-step plan myself. I've always been a little, uh, *soft* as a marshmallow role model, particularly when it's come to relationships. I am now fully committed to seeking only the mate who will be my marshmallow reward."

THE SIXTH STEP

What is your marshmallow dream? How will you achieve it? I strongly believe that the Five-Step Marshmallow Plan will lead to success in any endeavor, at any age and in any circumstance. But I want to add one more to the list:

Persevere. Do not give up. When Harry Collins, a super salesman, was asked how many calls he would make to a prospect before giving up, he said, "It depends on which one of us dies first."

. . .

When it's a marshmallow you care about—and it doesn't matter if it's a pair of shoes, a more rewarding love life or financial independence—delayed gratification can and will become an exciting challenge rather than an impossible chore. Practice the lessons preached in this book. I promise . . . marshmallow mountains will soon be yours.

Author Note

Although Jonathan Patient is a fictitious character, the marshmallow experiment in which he said he participated was quite real. Similarly, the stories about Larry Bird and Jorge Posada, ascribed to Jonathan, are based on real-life observations by Joachim de Posada. He found Larry Bird practicing alone on a basketball court when he was working as a team motivator for the Bucks (and had hoped to find a Milwaukee player in Bird's place). Jorge Posada (the New York Yankees removed the "de" from his name) is Joachim's cousin.

Some of the principles described are based on real experiences or observations by Joachim. His career in the Learning Systems Division of Xerox Corporation and as a motivational speaker in many countries taught him valuable lessons he has now shared with you.